75¢

W9-BCL-428

DISCOVERING TODAY'S CHINA

The Stubborn Land

DISCOVERING TODAY'S CHINA

City People, City Life
Posters and Pedicarts
The Stubborn Land
Youth on the March

Hardbound books distributed by
Creative Educational Society, Inc.;
Softbound by EMC Corporation.

The Stubborn Land

By Norman Webster
Peking Correspondent, 1969-1971
The Globe and Mail,
Toronto, Ontario, Canada

EMC Corporation
St. Paul, Minnesota

Library of Congress Cataloging in Publication Data

Webster, Norman, 1941-
    The stubborn land.

    (His Discovering today's China)
    1. Agriculture — China (People's Republic of China, 1949-   ) —
Juvenile literature. I. Title.
HD2067.W33   338.1'0951   72-13913
ISBN 0-912022-34-5
ISBN 0-912022-46-9 (pbk)

Published by EMC Corporation, 180 East 6th Street, St. Paul, Minnesota 55101

0 9 8 7 6 5 4 3 2 1

dikes that hold back a river. Torches are still seen in the early morning gloom, for the work has gone on all night, and now another shift is arriving from nearby villages. Hundreds walk or hitch rides on donkey carts. Soon they too will descend to the job — a chilly one, a dirty one, but a job that brings security closer with each shovelful of earth.

China's size can be misleading. Although it is a little larger than the United States in area, only a little more than one-tenth of the country is cultivated. The rest is unsuitable for farming. China's people are not spread evenly across the land, but concentrated along the main river valleys and on the plains near the eastern coast. Ninety-five percent of the people live in the eastern half of the country.

They live a life that combines some modern elements with ancient Asian peasant traditions. There are tractors and combines, but most farm work is still done by human muscles. The billions of rice shoots for the country's main crop are planted by millions of men and women stooping in the mud of the paddy fields. Radio, newspapers and films bring the outside world to the villages, but most women still get their news while washing their clothes together in a nearby stream.

In most respects it is an existence better than the life their parents and forefathers knew. In the old days, peasant life in China was primitive, and often something of a horror. Flood and drought, insects and disease, bandits and war were part of every farmer's life, and often the crops he managed to grow went mainly to his landlord as rent. Mao Tse-tung heard the groans of the peasants and marched to power in China with their support.

The greatest change that has occurred under Mao's Communism is the collectivization of agriculture. Fields and equipment are no longer owned by individuals but by all members of a "people's commune" together. A typical commune may number anywhere from 20,000 to 60,000 people and include a large number of villages. Farmers and their wives, sons, and daughters work in the fields or pigpens as always, but now they are paid wages by the commune. Each family is allowed to keep a small private plot of land on which it grows vegetables for its own table or raises a pig or two and some chickens.

Wages are very low. An able-bodied farm worker in an ordinary commune might make $140 dollars a year. In richer areas wages are higher, in poorer areas lower; they vary according to the commune's output. A good part of a farmer's wage will come to him in the form of food, mainly rice.

That sounds like a very small payment for one's work, and in North American terms it is, but for Asia it's not bad. In addition, a Chinese peasant family lives in its own small but sturdy house, eats reasonably well from its private plot, receives free schooling for the children and health care which is almost free. In the old days there was no such care at any price. The wages are enough to provide a warm quilt and cotton padded clothes for the winter. And a family may, by saving, hope to buy a bicycle, a radio, a wristwatch, a flashlight or other modest consumer goods.

It is a frugal existence, but it has its rewards and comforts and contains hope for future generations. For the first time in Chinese history, life is secure on the stubborn land.

Farming on parade

Cabbages and cotton and rice
are what China is all about

China is still primarily a farming nation, and every Chinese knows it. The well-being of the country still depends on the success of the crops. Schools close so young people can help with planting or harvesting. Millions of city dwellers also find themselves sent to the countryside every year for a few weeks to transplant rice in the spring or swing sickles in the fall. In years when the harvest falls short of expectations, China imports grain — usually wheat — to help feed its people. Most of the wheat comes from Canada and Australia, but in 1972, for the first time, the government in Peking bought some wheat and corn from the United States.

Floats carrying giant models of
Chinese cabbages (left), cotton and
rice sweep through the streets of
Peking during the parade marking the
21st anniversary of Communist China.

There are few machines to aid either in sowing or harvesting in China. Most work is done by human arms and backs. Here peasants drag a load of wheat across a field. Both men and women do heavy field work.

Carrying her long straw broom, a peasant woman marches along a village lane on her way to a cleanup job.

Most Chinese wheat is grown in the more northerly areas of the country, while rice is the principal crop in the central and southern regions. Overall, far more rice is grown than wheat. Food grains are vital, making up nearly 80 per cent of the Chinese diet. Scarcely anyone eats a meal whose main component is not rice or noodles or bread or some other grain product.

Sheltered by the broad brim of his straw hat, a peasant hoes his commune's fields.

Women swing mattocks to break up earth frozen by the cold winter of north China. Spring planting will soon follow.

Using a shoulder pole, a girl and a man carry away heavy rocks from a canal construction site. When the canal is finished, it will provide water for the crops.

It is vitally important for China to intro-
duce new farming techniques if it is to
feed its ever-growing population, already
by far the largest in the world. More and
more agricultural technicians are being
trained in modern methods. More and
more land is being farmed. New and better
seeds are being introduced.

**Young farmers intently follow a lesson in the field.
They learn mostly by practice rather than from books.**

Water buffalo are still very common in China, especially in the south. They pull ploughs in the muddy paddy fields and wagons on the dusty roads. Often they are tended by boys, who take them for swims in the large irrigation ditches. The animals lie sleepily in the water while their young masters splash and shout and climb on their backs. Water buffalo are owned by the members of a village collectively, not by individual families.

Shiny red tractors are starting to replace the big black water buffalo in some places. There aren't many yet, and it will be a long time before each of China's villages has one, but slowly and steadily Chinese agriculture is being mechanized.

It is harvest time, and at a commune near Peking a mechanical thresher roars and vibrates as it digests the wheat which the field hands feed it. The thresher separates the wheat into bags of grain and piles of straw.

People's communes also have small factories which produce farm tools and other items used by the rural people. Here women in blue coveralls pour molten iron into a mold. The iron will be used to make tools.

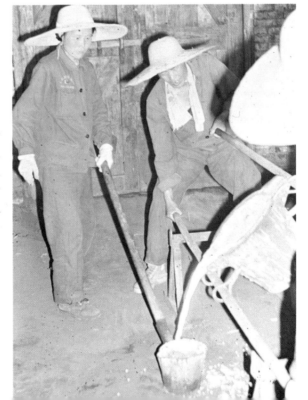

Each rural village has its tradesmen. Here a carpenter with an old-fashioned saw is working to produce a simple table for a peasant family. He has few tools, but they are lovingly cared for.

Peasant homes have very little furniture. A table and a chair are about all for most. Clothes are kept in trunks.

Holsteins with their black and white patches graze contentedly at a commune near Shanghai. But cows are not common in China. The country does not eat much beef, and it does not drink much milk. The most common farm animals are pigs and chickens.

The lady and her husband live in this single room.
About one-third of the floor space is taken up by the
oven-bed on which she is sitting; known as a *k'ang,*
it is heated in winter by a fire built underneath. The
cave contains only several big tubs for storing corn,
millet grain, wheat and potatoes, containers for
cooking oil, salt and sugar, a small wooden table and
rough dresser, a wood stove, pots, some small hand-
towels and a thermos for hot water. There is a picture
of Chairman Mao on the wall.

Seas and rivers serve the people

Fishermen gather their harvest
in China's seas and inland waters

Boats are important in China for fishing as well as carrying goods.
Some communes make their living from the sea. Fish are also caught
inland. Rivers, streams and canals yield harvests of fish, and most
villages have ponds where carp are raised.

China's inland waterways traditionally have been the nation's main highway, and the Communist regime has added many more miles to the network in the past 20 years. It is estimated that there are now more than 100,000 miles of navigable inland waterways in China, four times as many miles as there are in the railway network. The Yangtze River is the key transportation route to the interior of China.

A boat sets off to market with a load of cabbages.

Mao's peasant upbringing gave him strengths

China is a nation of peasants. Even the country's crafty old leader, Mao Tse-tung, is from a farming family. Mao didn't like peasant life very much. His father made him sweat in the fields when he wanted to read and study, but the physical strength he acquired has carried him through a lifetime of war and political struggle. And what he learned about peasant psychology enabled him to rouse China's farmers and their families to back him in his revolution.

This is the house of the Mao family in Shaoshan, Hunan province, southwest China. Here Mao Tse-tung was born on December 26, 1893. He grew up in Shaoshan, attending school in a nearby building and swimming in the pond in front of the house.

China has built
many dams in recent
years — for flood
control, water storage
and hydro-electric
power. Many peasant
houses now have an
electric light-bulb
hanging from the
ceiling.

A peasant girl carries her baby brother.
The women in the background work in a cotton
field outside Shanghai.

Terraced fields climb up a rough hillside in the Yellow River valley.

Chinese farmers make terraces to grow crops
in steep places which otherwise would yield
nothing. It is hard work. Many tons of rocks
and soil have to be brought in carts or baskets
and placed by hand to build up the terraces.

Although northern China has long, cold
winters, the most southerly portions of the
country are actually in the tropics and are hot
the year round. The fields yield two and
sometimes three crops of rice, and such
delicacies as sugar cane and bananas are also grown.

In Yenan, in northwest China, people actually live in caves cut into mountains of hard-packed silt. This is very practical. The caves are cool in summer and well sheltered from the bitter winds of winter. And they allow all the precious flat land below to be used to grow crops. On the left, an old man with his pipe stands outside the built-up entrance to a cave.

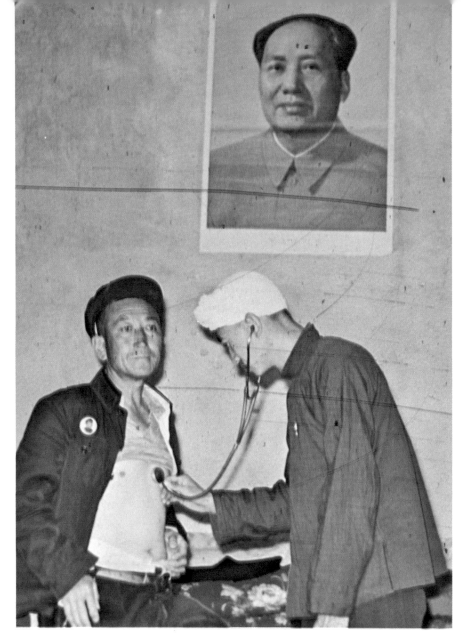

Inside one of the caves, under a portrait of Chairman Mao, Dr. Feng Chih-jen checks a patient's heart. Feng is one of the "barefoot doctors" who bring basic medical care to China's rural people. (They are called "barefoot doctors" because they go right into the wet rice fields alongside the peasants.) This man does not have nearly as much training as a North American doctor, but he can handle most of the peasants' day-to-day medical needs — treatment of cuts, broken bones, common illnesses, childbirth and so on.

Children play at the doorway of one of the cave homes. They live on the outskirts of Yenan, a rural town in northwest China which was Mao Tse-tung's headquarters from 1937-47 while fighting the Japanese and the Chinese Nationalists. These cave homes usually have only one room, which the whole family shares.

Rivers that once killed millions
are being tamed and channeled

Water control is the key to rural security. Over the centuries Chinese farmers have been plagued regularly by flood and drought. The Yellow River once was known as "China's sorrow" — and with good reason. Records going back more than 3,000 years show there were inundations or breaches in its dikes more than 1,500 times. These floods killed thousands, sometimes hundreds of thousands, directly. What is worse, they brought famines in which millions starved to death. Under the Communists, China has built dams, cut new paths for the waterways, and built canals to take the precious water to areas that used to be parched. The men on the next page are working on the Red Flag Canal project.

A country boy leads his donkey along the road. The donkey is pulling a barrel filled with human waste which will be spread on the fields to help the crops grow. Human manure is still vitally important to Chinese agriculture. It is carefully saved, even in the cities, and taken to the fields. Pig manure is important, too.

In the background of this picture is the doorway to a cave house.

Future farmers inspect their village's fields and water.

Below, two peasants
with portable tanks
spray a vegetable crop
with pesticides to kill
harmful bugs. More
pesticides are being
produced in China
these days, and more
chemical fertilizers.
The result is larger,
healthier crops.

Above, shoppers buy vegetables at a rural market. No one person owns this store. It is run by the state, which fixes the prices of the goods on sale. Peasants have small private plots of land on which they can raise their own vegetables and perhaps a pig or two. These they may eat themselves or sell to the state.

A peasant woman spreads grain out to dry.

On the left, a man
pulls water up from
his village's well.
Peasant homes do not
have running water.
Usually, families draw
from a neighborhood
pump.

The group in the picture
below lives in a com-
mune near Shanghai.
One man has a bicycle;
this is a major purchase
for a Chinese peasant.

This man's name is Liu Shu-shan. He is secretary of the Communist Party branch in the Shuang Wang production brigade in northwest China. The brigade has 1,812 members. Liu does not spend much time sitting behind a desk, but takes his turn regularly in the fields.

Groups of performers travel around the villages of China to
entertain the peasants. They sing and dance, warble a little
Peking Opera, do juggling, magic tricks and acrobatics. Here a
group performs in northwest China. The men have white towels
around their heads, a custom among the peasants of the area.
They are singing about Chairman Mao.

An important element in China's plans for national defense is its militia. Most militiamen and women are peasants, trained right in their home villages. The shooting scores of the young people above indicate they would be strong defenders of their native land.

The girl on the right is Tsou Yu-fung, 21, a "revolutionary story teller" in a village near Yenan, northwest China. The village story teller is an institution in China. Miss Tsou continues the tradition, although she adds Chairman Mao and the Communist Party to the familiar tales of good and evil, horror and salvation.